WHAT I WOULD SAY.........

IF

I WERE AN EVANGELIST

ISBN **978061519372 4**

For Carlos, Claude and Camille

Claudine Cheatem is a fresh new writer. She has unique and innovative ways to get her point across. Her writing is down to earth and will be appreciated for many generations to come. We need Claudine's in the face approach to life. I look forward to reading more from her.

Marie Brock Tinsley

FORWORD

Do you feel like you are living under a dark cloud? As if you have exhausted all your resources and nothing is changing? To look at you, most folks wouldn't know that you are a shell of a person. You look like you could be on the cover of "Got It Going On" magazine. But you are empty inside. The voice inside you is silent. And when it does speak, it tells you what a mess you have made of your life and lives of the people that you love. You have even entertained the thought that your life is no longer worth living.

I can relate to all of that, because I was there once. It was at a point in my life when nothing seemed to be going right. I was in a dysfunctional marriage, and it didn't have hopes of getting better. So every night for almost 2 months I prayed, "Please God, don't let me wake up tomorrow. Just withdraw the breathe from my body, don't make me have to jump in front of a moving car or take a bunch of pills. Just withdraw your breathe from my body, then no one will have to know how miserable I am on the inside. Well, I thank God that I will never know if He would answer a prayer like that, but one day the opportunity to answer my own prayer presented itself to me in such a way that I was forced to make a life-saving decision.. I was driving I-35 south to Kansas City, MO. I was driving at least 75 miles an hour, with the intent to pass the car in front of me. As I entered the driver's blind spot, he suddenly decided he wanted to drive in the same lane I was in. I immediately slammed on the brakes, which caused the car to do a series of 360 degrees turns in the middle of the highway. My voice inside of me was screaming to God "This is not what I asked you for. I said me, not my mother, not my brother, not my children." All the while I was talking to God I was fighting to gain control of the car, and thereby save my life. Not for my sake but for the sake of my mother, my brother and my three small children that were riding with me. I fought to live to save someone else's life. And it worked. My son is now a youth counselor and my brother is the proud father of 4 beautiful children. What I want you to understand is that your life is not all about you. The breath you breathe, the moves you make, and your life experiences are not all about you. It's about the people around you. Someone's destiny is *tied directly to YOU! If I had succeeded in getting an answer to my selfish prayer I would not be here today to speak words of encouragement to you. I can't tell you how to make it through the next 5, 10, 15 years of your life. But for today, GET UP. Make a phone call, visit a friend, volunteer at the homeless shelter, go visit the sick. Fight for your life, if not for your sake...for the sake of the person that needs you. And in doing so, you will find true purpose and will in turn learn to love the life that you live.*

ACKNOWLEDGEMENTS

I have complied some messages that I hope will encourage you to never give up. The human spirit has moxie. Quitting is never an option.

I appreciate the life lessons that I learned though the example of my parents, Orange and Martha Cheatem. Neither had any formal education beyond high school, but the task of being the parents of 15 children put the PHD behind their names. The cloth that I was cut from was weaved with integrity, honesty, and a work ethic that could only be found in the chaos and conflict of what I called home. For that I am eternally grateful.

Daddy, you use to tell me that I think too fast and I talk too much. Well Daddy, I am going to slow my thought process, close my mouth and write some of my thoughts down.
Mom, you would always say, "If I can get you to listen to me, I can help you." Well Mom, if you only knew how crystal clear your voice is to me now. I am listening.

To the both of you, your labor has not been in vain.

I would also like to acknowledge someone that God used as an instrument to pour into my mind some of the best spiritual theatrics and one-liners. Dr. Jeremiah Reed, if it were not for the mental recollection of you in the pulpit, leg raised slapping the pulpit, hand behind your ear as you yelled out the word of God, I would have let go. I still have yet to see the smoky presence of the Holy Ghost hover over a man as it did when you were preaching. Great is thy reward.

Table of Contents

A DIAMOND IN THE ROUGH

A diamond is the one of the most sought after gems on the earth. Diamond comes from the Greek word adamas, which means indestructible. It's brilliance and unsurpassed beauty is often compared to the woman. The true value of a diamond is never determined until it has been through the stages of perfection. It is unfinished, imperfect and has not been refined, polished or prepared. Just as a diamond's true value is not known while it is in its "rough" stage, so it is with a woman that has not been redeemed, justified and sanctified by the Lord.

There are some amazing facts regarding a diamond that I would like to share with you.

Diamonds and graphite (the lead in a pencil) are made from the same element, carbon.

One is cheap and used by everyone and the other is the most valuable material on the earth and admired by everyone. The way carbon responds to the heat and pressure during the perfection process determines if it will become a diamond or a pencil lead. Proverbs 14:1 Every wise woman buildeth her house, but the foolish plucketh it down with her hands.

Your response to the pressures of life, your reaction to the disappointments and the letdowns determines your position. The "eth" at the end of a word indicates that continual process, motion, or effort is required. So you must be in continual motion to build, to construct, to put together your life. If you are not in the building process, you will be in a continual process of living a self-defeating, worthless life. To pluck means to pull out by strands. To put that in terms of your life, it means that you are, with everything decision you make, you are slowly bringing your life down to nothing. The intimate relationships that you drift in and out of. The alcohol and drugs you abuse. The cigarettes you smoke. The way you handle your money. All of these things lead to a life that is riddled with unnecessary toil and strife.

Proverbs 24:3 Through wisdom a house is built, and by understanding it is established.

Wisdom is a wise plan from God. Understanding is how to execute that plan. Now I can't tell you what the specific plan for your life is, but I can tell you that God has one for you. In order for you know God's plan for your life and your house, you need to become more acquainted with Him. Ask Him to make Himself known to you.

To build means to form or to devise by fitting parts or elements together systematically. God will work all things, every heartache and disappointment He will systematically fit it all together for your good.

Another interesting fact regarding the diamond is that the best place to find a new diamond mine is next to an old diamond mine.

Titus 2:3-4 That the aged women likewise, that they be in behavior that becometh holiness, not false accusers, not given to much wine, teachers of good things; that they teach the younger women to be sober, to love their husbands to love their children.

There is nothing more beautiful than a mature woman that has found her place in Christ and is able to reach out to a younger woman and help her find her place in Christ. But by the same token there is nothing more disgusting than a young woman with no class, no manners, no grace. We are missing it somewhere, ladies, it's time to lift up the standard.

Two things have to happen for this to become reality 1) the younger women have to have teachable spirits - open to correction and willing to change. 2) The older women have to know how to teach in the spirit of meekness, not so you can be glorified - but with Godly wisdom, so you can see the will of God done in the younger woman's life.

Colossians 4:6 Let your conversation always be with grace, seasoned with salt, that you may know how you ought to answer each one.

You know what salt does - it stops the decay - so when your words are seasoned they are able to stop the decay of sin and degradation in one's life. Salt also preserves - saves for future use- your words and the example that you set as an older woman will help save someone from the snares of this world. Make a commitment to yourself that you will be an instrument that God can use to help a younger woman find her purpose in Him.

Every diamond has what is known as a gem print. This is a unique reflection and refraction pattern the diamond emits when low-level light strikes the top of the stone. The likelihood of two identical gem prints is about the same likelihood of finding two identical fingerprints.

Psalm 139:14 I will praise thee, for I am fearfully and wonderfully made.

You are one of a kind. Your unique personality sparkles and dazzles people when you are a reflection of His light.

You may be in the rough stage of your life, but it is never to late to let the Lord do his work and bring out the brilliance of the diamond that is within you. You have to go thru the process of being polished, refined and finished.

To be polished means to be improved by removing crudeness or vulgarity.

Colossians 3: 8 But now you yourselves are to put off all these: anger, wrath, malice, blasphemy, filthy language out of your mouth.

Learn how to express yourself with eloquence. I'm not saying to learn big words so that you can impress people, but there other words besides the one syllable four letter ones that can express your frustration, enthusiasm, joy or any other emotion you are experiencing. The words that come out of your mouth will either command someone's attention, or will fall on deaf ears. It's all about presentation.

To be refined is to be free from impurities or imperfections.

I Thess 5:22 Flee the very appearance of evil.

To be prepared is to be made ready for a specific purpose.

2 Cor 5:18 Now all things are of God, who has reconciled us to Himself and has given to us the ministry of reconciliation.

To be finished is to put final touches on.

Esther 5:1 Now it happened on the third day that Esther put on her royal robes and stood in the inner court of the king's palace.

To be perfected is to be in a condition of complete excellence. Excellence always exalts the Lord; arrogance exalts you and your agenda.

When Queen Esther knew that she was going to present herself to the King, she put effort into the way she looked. She wanted to present herself as a classy woman that commanded respect. She was a woman on a mission and she didn't want to be mistaken for anything less. She caught the attention of the King and her petitions were heard and granted. It was due in great part to the way she carried herself.

In all of its brilliance and alluring beauty a diamond is actually just a stone that, after it has withstood the pressure and heat, is able to reflect light.
A Godly woman is just a female that has withstood the pressures and heat of life and is able to reflect the love and light of Christ. Think of Coretta Scott King. Need I say more?
This is my last point. A misdirected blow from the diamond cutter's mallet can shatter a diamond into rubble, with no salvage

value. This fact separates the woman from the diamond. It makes her, in the lowest condition of her life, more valuable than the most expensive diamond on the earth. A shattered diamond can quickly be swept away, discarded as useless, but as a woman your life can never be too shattered or too broken to be repaired by the master jeweler's hand.

Jeremiah 29:11 For I know the thoughts that I think towards you, saith the Lord, thoughts of peace, and not evil, to give you an expected end.

It does not matter what you have experienced in your life; if it is not the end that God has planned for you, things have to improve. Although, a diamond can be considered worthless because of its flaws, you as a woman are indestructible. There is more "eth" left in you. Use it to build your life.

LAUNCH OUT INTO THE DEEP

Please read Luke 5:1-9. It will help you to grasp the essence of what I am about to say.

In this passage of scripture, Jesus notices that the ship was not being used to its full potential. It sat idle on the edge of the water. Barely getting wet, when in fact it was designed to sail and conquer the deepest of waters. Jesus entered into the vessel and then commanded the person in charge to launch out into the deep. This shows the willingness of Jesus to use a vessel, but at the same time, He is not going to overpower the person that should be in charge. You are in charge of your life. You are expected to take the wheel and navigate it over the sea of life. However, the Lord will guide you through the rough spots.

Simon Peter is a lot like most of us. The first thing that comes to mind when it time to take on a great task is all of the defeats that we have previously encountered. We get flashbacks of all the mistakes that we have made. Sometimes we talk ourselves into just staying idle on the shore. That's where it safe. At least you know you can't sink as long as you are tied to the shore. But Jesus told him to "Launch out into the deep and let down your nets for a draught."

Let me break down these words and then spoon-feed them to you.

launch - to set forth with some force, to throw oneself into something with vigor

out - beyond a normal condition

deep - extremely grave or serious

let - to give the use of, to allow, to permit

nets - anything that ensnares, anything left over after certain deductions
  or allowances

draught - see draft or draw

draft - the choosing or taking of an individual from a group for a special purpose

draw - to pull out to the fullest extent, a written order issued by one person
  directing the payment to another person

Can you tell where I'm going with this? It is time to quit being idle and let God use you to your fullest potential. How many times have you poured your heart out to God? How many times have you told Him all about your mistakes, your failed attempts, your short comings, your this or your that? He hears you but His answer will still be "Launch out into the deep."

After you have beat up on yourself, after you have contradicted Him and told Him what He is wanting you to do will never work. After you have told yourself you are not worthy, after you get through making excuses about your situation, and when you get through blaming other people. What do you have left? Just a little bit of strength? Just a little bit of faith? God is telling you to take the "net of your will" and with such force and vigor stat on some new course. Something beyond your normal condition, into a more grave and serious matter. Put away anything that ensnares or traps you and allow whatever is in your possession to be used by God. Knock on that door again. Apply for that job again. Apply for that scholarship again – you know what it is that you are just about to give up on. Well, God is saying do it again – Launch out into the deep!!!!!1

You have been drafted, chosen, called out from the group of your peers, for God's special purpose. Prepare yourself to be pulled to the fullest extent, to be used to your fullest potential.

God has written an order directing payment to you. In order to direct payment or write a draft one has to have access to or authority over that resource. Christ is our access. He sits at the right hand of the Father and makes intercession for us. He also has the authority, because all power in heaven and in earth has been given unto Him. The earth is His footstool.

Whatever your specific need is, I want you to know that you have a resource that you are not using to the fullest potential. Alexis Carrel said, "Prayer, our deepest source of power and perfection, has been left miserably undeveloped."

Each of you should examine yourself to find out if you are that vessel, just idling at the shoreline of life. Fashion in your heart what

it is going to take for you to follow the
instructions of the Lord.   Whatever the
Lord has said to you, acknowledge it. Write
down what you are going to do to launch out
into the deep. Finish school. Write that
play. Start that business. Whatever it is,
write it down and reference back to this as
the day you renewed yourself and your
commitments to God. You will notice in the
scripture it says, "after they had done this".
Not while they were lying in bed thinking
about doing it, or while they were waiting
for someone else to get started. Not while
they were waiting for the weather to change.
Not while they were thinking about how
funny their money was. But "AFTER THEY
HAD DONE THIS". That's when they were
able to cash in on the draft that Jesus had
written. The reason their nets were so full is
that Jesus had commanded the fish into their
nets. There are some blessings that Jesus has
commanded just for you. Throw out your
nets. You can't comprehend the draft that

Jesus has written for your life. The word says he is able to do exceedingly abundantly above all that you could ask or think. The blessings that He will bestow upon you are so bountiful there will be more than enough to share with others. You will be blessed to be a blessing.

You have been called for a special purpose and until you get about doing that you will always relate to the disciple's first experience "Master we have toiled all the night and have taken nothing." Aren't you tired of coming up empty handed? Aren't you tired of working overtime and still not having enough? Aren't you tired of sitting idle? Don't you want to relate to the disciple's second experience? You are the head of the ship, take control of the wheel and "launch out into the deep and prepare yourself for the bountiful haul."

THE DOOR TO ANSWERED PETITIONS

So many times we take certain requests to the Lord and we wonder why after all of our snot slinging, hand wringing and hooping and hollering we don't always get the answer we want.

I John 5:14-15 And this is the confidence that we have in Him, that if we ask anything according to His will, He heareth us: And if we know that He hear us, whatsoever we ask, we know that we have the petitions the we desired of Him.

Anyone that writes grant proposals know that there is a process that one goes through before the final proposal is submitted for approval. One of the most important aspects of the process is the research. So it is when we petition the Lord. In our daily lives we should never forget just how awesome He is and what a privilege it is to appear before

Him with our requests. When we approach
Him with a request we should be more
reverential than we are to the mortgage
banker. When you are trying to get that loan
to go through on your home, you are polite
and respectful and very cooperative. Well,
you don't have to kiss up to the Lord. He
doesn't need your praise and reverence - HE
DESERVES IT!!!

I'm not saying that you have to approach
God with big words. He understands your
language, whether you speak Ebonics or
Latin. But I think as a generation, we have
lost a reverential fear of God. Give Him the
honor and praise that He is due as you
present your petitions to Him.
Solomon is a good example of this.

II Chron 1:9-10 Now O, Lord God, let thy
promise unto David my father be established:
for thou hast made me king over a people like
the dust of the earth in multitude. Give me

now wisdom and knowledge, that I may go out and come in before this people: for who can judge this thy people, this is so great?

Solomon knew the God of his father was a God that could not lie. There was no need ask for a whole bunch of "stuff." Solomon knew there were promises that God had made and if those things came to pass in his life he would have everything that he needed. So his prayer was "help me to keep a level head, when you start blessing me."

There are promises that God has made concerning you and your family. You don't have to start asking for cars, houses, jobs and all the usual stuff we clutter our prayer life with. God is a promise keeper. All you need to do is make sure you know what the promises are so that when they start coming to past, you will know that it was God that did it and not you.

But still, there are times when we ask God for things. And that is okay, because He is our heavenly Father. We go to Him with our heavy hearts and with our broken spirits.

When Hannah wanted a baby she went to God with her petition. Her husband couldn't understand why he couldn't make her happy. But she knew that she could go to God with her innermost secrets and reveal her pain to Him. When no one else understands your dreams and your desires you can take them to God. You don't have to settle for what someone else wants you to have, go to God with your petition.

I Sam 1:10 *And she was in bitterness of soul, and prayed unto the Lord and wept sore.*

King David prayed to God concerning his sick child.

II Sam 12:16 David therefore sought the Lord for the child; and David fasted and went in and lay all night upon the earth.

Although this was the child that was conceived in adultery, David still knew that He could go to God and ask for his child to be healed. David was so secure in his relationship with God that he knew in the midst of his mess, he could still call on God. When you can go to someone and say "I know I messed up, but I need your help" that shows love, respect and reverence.

But in all that we do and all that we pray for, we still have to wait on the answer. What if God grants your petition? What if He doesn't?
After Hannah poured out her heart to God, the king told her that her petition had been granted. The scripture says that she went her way and did eat and her countenance was no longer sad. Your countenance is the way you

are feeling on the inside showing all over your face. You don't have to say a word. Have you ever known someone that was going thru hell, but it doesn't show on his or her face. When they start telling you about what they are facing you be like "Girl, I would have never guessed that you are going thru that. You look so happy." The circumstances may not change, but when you get the answer from God, you change. And you go on with life. Although Hannah did not have a baby yet, there was a promise made to her, and that was the same as if she was rocking a baby in her arms at that moment. She went on to the house, did what she had to do with her husband and the scripture said, "Hannah conceived a baby." How we all love happy endings.

Now King David's outcome is another story. II Sam 12: 19-20 But when David saw that his servants whispered, David perceived that the child was dead: therefore David said unto his servants, Is the child dead? And

they said, He is dead. Then David arose from
the earth, washed, and anointed himself and
changed his apparel, and came into the house
of the Lord and worshipped: then he came to
his own house; and when he required, they
set bread before him and he did eat.
Both David and Hannah requested a child of
the Lord. Both went before the Lord and
poured out their hearts to Him. Both
received an answer but they were different.
You would think that since they got two
different answers that they would have
responded in two different ways, but they
didn't. They both went on with their lives,
serving and praising and giving glory to God.
There is much to be learned from these two.
Hannah received a promise that her petition
had been granted. But if she would have ran
all over town quoting scriptures, talking
about what God said He was going to do and
had never done what is required to conceive a
child, she would have missed out on her
petition. King David poured out his heart

with the same intensity and same hurt that Hannah did, yet his answer was no. Until you are ready to hear "no" from God, you are not ready to do His will. "Yes, dear is not the only answer you will get from God. Even after a solemn fast and making sacrifices you might still hear no. And what do you do then? The same thing King David did. You rise from the earth, which is nothing more than your selfish desires and wants - get to the house of the Lord and worship. You continue to do what is required of you. We have to get to the point that we can say, "Blessed be the name of the Lord" in all situations.

We often tell the different Bible stories as if the characters were made up by Dr. Seuss are good bedtime stories. But of a surety King David lived and experienced what is written as did Hannah and Solomon. The same God that they petitioned is the same God that we cry out to. And just as sure as God answered them so will He answer you. We don't serve a god that has been carved in stone or fashioned from gold. We serve a God whose eyes are beholding us, His ears are inclined to us, His hand is outstretched to us, and His angels are encamped about us all day. What a mighty God we serve!!!!!

IT'S TIME FOR A CHANGE

Acts 3:1-10 Acts 4:22

The scripture say this man was lame from his mother's womb and was carried. This is interesting to me, because I don't know anyone that comes out of the womb knowing how to walk. So to me, it means from his mother's womb people had put limitations on him. Lame means crippled or disabled. It also means to be poor, unconvincing weak and ineffective.

All of these were labels that other people had put on him. He was told from the time he could understand human language "you can't walk. Let other people carry you." So he sunk into the mold that other people had made for him. He sat at the gate and begged for alms - the very food he ate, the clothes he wore, the money he had was all determined by the strangers that he encountered day to day.

People actually took this man and laid him at the gate of the temple, which was called Beautiful. This is like taking a Sunday drive looking at all the beautiful homes, then going back to your little shack, because in your mind people like you don't live in houses like that.

I can imagine the church folks looked at this man and thought "O, that's sister so n so's boy. Girl, he been crippled all his life poor little thing. Here let me reach in my coach bag and give him a dollar or two. Cause that's all he needs. He aint going nowhere, he aint doing nothing."

But inside this man wanted more. He wanted to do more, but his mistake was that he thought his destiny was tied up in people. But one thing he had that helped to change his life was expectancy. He expected somebody to give him food, clothes and money. In his mind he was someone in need of a handout. But one day, his expectancy and his destiny collided.

Peter told him "in the name of Jesus Christ of Nazareth rise up and walk."

The names of all the folks that had spoken gloom and dome over him, that had looked at him like he was a reject, that had thought he wasn't worth their time, all of their names and their words and the negative effects they had on his life were at that moment like a vapor in the wind.

Acts 3:8 And he leaping up stood, and walked and entered with them into the temple, walking and leaping and praising God.

Acts 4:22 For the man was forty years old, on whom this miracle of healing was shewed.

For forty years this man was in this condition, but it changed. Forty years he had to endure the stares and the smirks of folks. Forty years he had to ask folks to contribute to his very existence. Forty years of begging for just enough to make it though the day. Couldn't put one foot in front of the other and stay on balance. Other people dictated where he was going and how he was going to get there. When he got too heavy, they dropped him off. Tired of carrying him, tired of supporting him. But one day, someone with the knowledge of what Christ could do for him hit him right between the eyes.

The wonderful thing about this is that immediately his feet and anklebones received strength. The same feet that folks had probably stepped on and the same anklebones that could not support his weight received strength.

The amazing thing about this man is that he leaped up and walked and leaped and praised his way all the way into the temple. I'm sure he passed some of the same folks that had carried him and left him at the gate.

The disciples did not have to drag him into the temple. He went with them. Why? Because that is where his hearts desire was. The leap was in him.

What is it that has been plaguing your life? Are you sick in your body? Are you going thru another bankruptcy? Are you going thru another divorce? Lost another job? Evicted again? Can't shake that addiction? I'm telling you that there is a leap in you that even forty years of being in the same condition can't stop the leap in you. In the name of Jesus Christ of Nazareth, I say to you "Rise up and walk." It is time for a change.

Rise Up, Stretch Out and Come Forth

I went to a comedy show in Kansas City a couple of years ago. As I was sitting there cracking up, almost to the point of falling on the floor...something happened. I saw an auditorium full of people, so in the need of some kind of escapism that they were willing to pay somebody to make them laugh. I wasn't very much impressed with the next comedian so I walked into the lobby. There was a young man standing at the product table of the comedian that just had me cracking up. This was the saddest looking young man I had seen in a while. He just looked broken. I wanted to tell him, "You need to go in there and listen to that show so you can laugh some." But then I realized it was the comedian that had just left the audience in stitches. All I could think about was the song by Smokey Robinson and the Miracles "The tears of a Clown."

We encounter people everyday, like the comedian, who are doing whatever to mask the real pain in their lives. People whose lives have withered up, whose future appears to be dead. People hiding behind laughter, drugs, alcohol and other things rather than deal with real life situations. Well, Jesus can make a difference in any situation. It doesn't matter how hopeless or how dark things look. The story in Luke the 6th chapter introduces us to a man with a withered up right hand. Please read the story. I can imagine this man got up and thought it was going to be life as usual as he struggled to get dressed with his withered up hand. But in the course of his day, he encountered Jesus. Here he is with his withered up hand, and Jesus gone put him on blast in front of all those folks. Not only did He call him out; make him stand in front of all those people. At this time, I'm sure the man is embarrassed and his withered up hand has never in his mind been so ugly. I'm sure as he was standing up, he was thinking of an answer. He just knew Jesus was going to ask him "What happened to your hand." He had his answer "See, Jesus. What had happened was. . ." But to his surprise, Jesus does something even more puzzling. He said unto the man "stretch forth thy hand." When the man stretched forth his hand it was restored as whole as the other.

So many times we allow our selves to get withered up. Webster defines withered as dried up as by heat. We allow the pressure and the heat of life to make us withdraw. We lose our vigor, our freshness. We become stale and dried up. Every time you start something big or new in your life, there are a bunch of folks standing around telling you why you can't do that. So many are eager to point out your shortcomings. They didn't even call this man by his name. He was just known as "the man with the withered up hand". What are people calling you? Do they see you as the one that will never amount to nothing? Are you the one that can't complete what they start? When you focus on Jesus and what He is saying, you will be able to see life and strength renewed in what you allowed to become withered up. Then you will be able to stand in the midst of a bunch of folks that don't have any confidence in you and see your withered up situation made whole.

But what if you're not just withered up? What if you are just going thru the motions of life but there is no life in you? Even when you have surveyed your whole life and declare it to be hopeless there is always hope in Jesus. He can even bring life to a dead thing.

John 11:25 Jesus said unto her "I am the resurrection and the life: he that believeth in me though he were dead yet shall he live.

When something is dead the most appropriate thing to do is to bury it. Cry your tears and try to move on. But what if you're dead on the inside and you have tried to bury yourself. You bury yourself in your job, in nightclubs, volunteer work, drugs, alcohol and even church, but nothing is working. Your life seems to be a funeral. Just this unending sadness before the burial. How do you continue to go on? Let's read this scripture again.

John 11:25 Jesus said unto her "I am the resurrection and the life: he that believeth in me though he were dead yet shall he live.

Jesus was talking to Martha about her brother, who had actually died and had been buried. As a matter of fact, he had been dead about four days. But what did Jesus say? "He that believeth in me though he were dead, yet shall he live."

There is no situation in this life that you can present to Jesus that He does not have the answer for. He is the answer. I can imagine Lazarus lying there...dead, lifeless, no future. He was nothing but a used to be in everybody's eyes. Now all they could say was what Lazarus coulda shoulda woulda done.

So has everyone counted you out? Who has cast you aside as a could have been, or a should have been? Who looks at you and thinks your future is dead? There is always hope.
Even the very state of death had to step back when Jesus spoke.

John 11:43 And when He thus had spoken, He cried with a loud voice "Lazarus, come forth.

Although he was dead, Lazarus had no choice but to do like the man with the withered up hand. He had to move toward the voice of Jesus.

John 11:44 And he that was dead came forth.

People, there is always hope. That same Jesus that walked the earth and ascended into heaven is the same Jesus that is willing and able to make a difference in your life. But He works through men and women that have allowed Him to change their lives.

Mark 16: 19-20 So then after the Lord had spoken unto them He was received up into heaven, and sat on the right hand of God. And they went forth and preached everywhere, the Lord working with them and confirming the word with signs following. Amen.

Jesus is still seeking to save those that are lost. To heal them that are broken and bring life to a dead existence. He wants to place your feet on solid ground and bring balance to your life.

I know some of you are wondering where does my faith come from. You're wondering if I have ever been withered, dead on the inside or just off balance.

Where do you want me to start? Should I start at the point in my life when 3 young thugs stuck a 16-gauge shotgun to my daddy's chest and blew him away for $33.00? Should I start at the point where my mother died in my arms? Maybe I should start at my sixth eviction? Or my second bankruptcy? Or my second divorce?

Act3:16 "And His name through faith in his name hath made this man strong, whom you see and know: yeah the faith which is by *him hath given him this perfect soundness in the presence of you all.*

It doesn't matter where I start, because the conclusion of the matter is this. I have walked with Him, and talked with Him and I have allowed Him to intervene in my life. By His name and faith in His name this woman is strong and He has given me perfect soundness. So I can say to you "in the name of Jesus, rise up, stretch out and come forth". Let Jesus make a difference in your life.

www.ingramcontent.com/pod-product-compliance
Lightning Source LLC
Chambersburg PA
CBHW030305030426
42337CB00012B/590